D0319576

ANOTHER NIGHT
BEFORE CHRISTMAS

ANOTHER NIGHT BEFORE CHRISTMAS

Carol Ann Duffy

with illustrations by Rob Ryan

PICADOR

With many thanks to Liberty Wright

First published 2010 by Picador
an imprint of Pan Macmillan, a division of Macmillan Publishers Limited
Pan Macmillan, 20 New Wharf Road, London N1 9RR
Basingstoke and Oxford
Associated companies throughout the world
www.panmacmillan.com

ISBN 978-0-330-52393-6

1 3 5 7 9 8 6 4 2

A CIP catalogue record for this book is available from the British Library.

Typeset in Fournier and Futura
Manufactured in Belgium by Proost

Visit *www.picador.com* to read more about all our books and to buy them.
You will also find features, author interviews and news of any author events,
and you can sign up for e-newsletters so that you're always first
to hear about our new releases.

For Ella with love from Mummy

ANOTHER NIGHT
BEFORE CHRISTMAS

On the night before Christmas, a child in a house,
As the whole family slept, behaved just like a mouse . . .
And crept on soft toes down red-carpeted stairs.
Her hand held the paw of her favourite bear.

The Christmas tree posed with its lights in its arms,
Newly tinselled and baubled with glittering charms;
Flirting in flickers of crimson and green
Against the dull glass of the mute TV screen.

The hushed street was in darkness. Snow duveted the cars –
A stray cat had embroidered each roof with its paws.
An owl on an aerial had planets for eyes.
The child at the window stared up at the sky,

Where two aeroplanes sped to the east and the west,
Like a pulled Christmas cracker. The child held her breath
And looked for a sign up above, as the moon
Shone down like a gold chocolate coin on the town.

Far beyond the quiet suburbs, the motorway droned
As it cradled the drivers who murmured at phones
And drove through the small hours, this late Christmas Eve,
The ones who were faithless, the ones who believed.

But the child who was up and long out of her bed
Saw no visions of sugar plums dance in her head;
She planned to discover, for once and for all,
If Santa Claus (or Father Christmas) was real.

There were some who said no, he was really just Mum,
With big cushions or pillows to plump out her tum,
Or Dad, with a red cloak and cotton-wool beard,
A whisky or three down his neck for Good Cheer.

So she took up position behind a big chair
That was close to the fireplace. Four stockings hung there.
Quite soon there'd be one tangerine in each toe
And she'd be the child who would see and would know.

And outside, a lone taxi crunched back into town,
Where the shops had their shutters, like giant eyelids, down,
And people in blankets, with nowhere to go,
Were hunched in shop doorways to keep from the snow;

Where a giant plastic Santa climbed up the Town Hall
And security guards dozed or smoked in the Mall.
The cashpoints glowed softly, like icons of light,
From corner to corner, on Christmas Eve night.

Then a shooting star whizzed down the sky from the North.
It was fizzing and sparkling as it fell to earth,
And growing in size. A young hare in a field
Gazed up at the sky where it brightened and swelled.

It turned into a sleigh, made of silver and gold,
Pulled by reindeer, whose breath chiffoned out in the cold,
With bells on their antlers and bells round each hoof.
Then – clatter! – they landed on you-know-who's roof.

Now, herself near the fireplace had fallen asleep,
So she missed every word that a voice, warm and deep,
Was saying above her, as each reindeer's name
Was spoken, and flared in the night like a flame.

Dasher, whoa! Dancer, whoa! Prancer! Vixen! Well done!
Comet, whoa! Cupid, whoa! Donner! Blitzen! What fun!
The shadows of reindeer were patterns on snow
Which gift-wrapped the garden, three storeys below.

It's a fact that a faraway satellite dish,
Which observes us from space, cannot know what we wish.
Its eye's empty socket films famine and greed,
But cannot see Santa Claus on Christmas Eve.

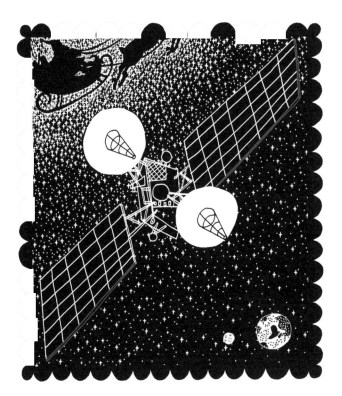

He was dressed all in red, from his head to his toes,
Also red was the Christmassy glow of his nose.
His beard was as white as the flakes that fell down
On rich and on poor in this ordinary town.

His eyes twinkled like tinsel and starlight and frost,
And they knew how to give without counting the cost.
He'd slung on his back a huge sackful of toys
To lug down the chimneys of good girls and boys.

Dasher snorted, and Blixen pawed hard at the roof –
They'd a long night before them, and that was the truth!
But Santa had vanished! A puff of black soot
Burped out of the chimney, dislodged by his foot.

All this noise woke the child, who had fallen asleep,
So she popped up her head and made sure she could peep
(Without being seen) at whoever it was
Who stood in the fireplace. Big Wow! Santa Claus!

Though she lived in an age where celebrity ruled
And when most of the people were easily fooled
By TV and fashion, by money and cars,
The little girl knew that here was a real STAR!

Then she watched as the room filled with magic and light
As the spirit of Christmas made everything bright
And suddenly presents were heaped by the tree –
But she didn't wonder, which ones are for me?

For the best gift of all is to truly believe
In the wonderful night that we call Christmas Eve,
When adults remember, of all childhood's laws,
This time in December will bring Santa Claus.

Santa turned and he winked at her, then disappeared,
With a laugh, up the chimney, with soot in his beard.
She ran to the window and watched as his sleigh
Took off from her roof and he sped on his way.

And as long as she lived she would never forget
How he flew, as the moon showed him in silhouette,
From rooftop to rooftop and called from his flight
HAPPY CHRISTMAS TO ALL AND TO ALL A GOOD NIGHT.

Also by Carol Ann Duffy and available from Picador

Carol Ann Duffy
Mrs Scrooge

A Christmas Tale